GROSS
BODY STUFF

Darla Duhaime

Educational Media

rourkeeducationalmedia.com

TABLE OF CONTENTS

HUMAN AND NOT-SO-HUMAN STUFF

Snot, eye goo, and gas. Poop, vomit, and ear wax. When it comes to gross stuff, the human body is full of it. It's also full of stuff that's not human.

GROSS ME

Your body has more microbial cells than human cells. Microbes are bacteria, viruses, and other single-cell organisms. The human body has about 10 trillion human cells. It has about 100 trillion microbial cells.

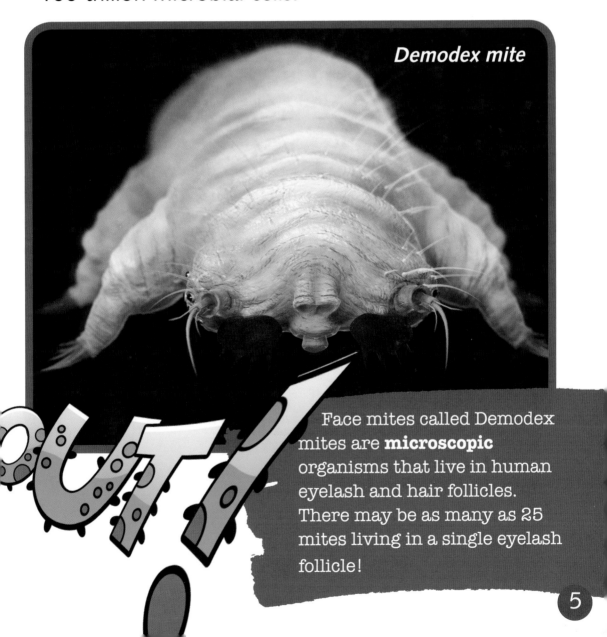

Demodex mite

Face mites called Demodex mites are **microscopic** organisms that live in human eyelash and hair follicles. There may be as many as 25 mites living in a single eyelash follicle!

What's that stuff doing in there? Most of these microscopic bugs that live in and on us actually keep us healthy.

Lactobacillus acidophilus is found in active yogurt cultures. This bacterium helps with digestion.

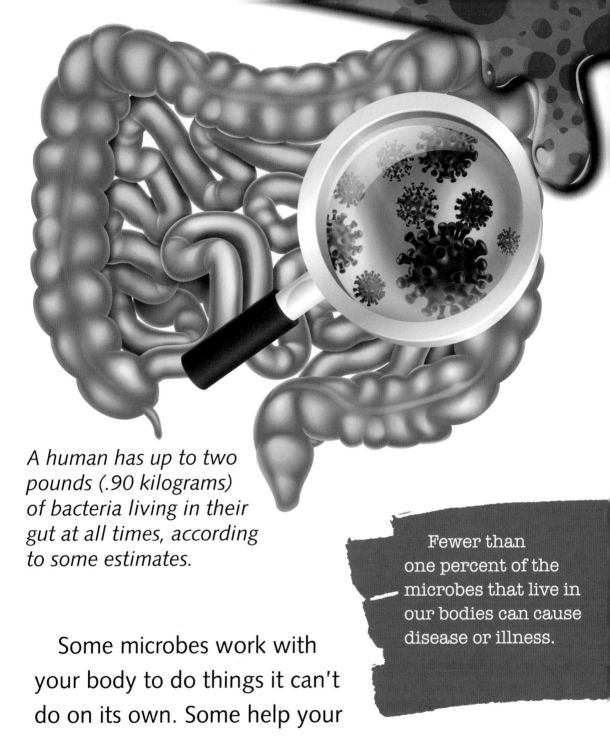

A human has up to two pounds (.90 kilograms) of bacteria living in their gut at all times, according to some estimates.

Fewer than one percent of the microbes that live in our bodies can cause disease or illness.

Some microbes work with your body to do things it can't do on its own. Some help your body digest food. Some fight against the bad viruses and bacteria that can make you sick.

WHAT STINKS?

When you smell something, it's because **molecules** from whatever you're smelling have made it into your nose.

Smell that poopy diaper? Guess what that means!

On average, a person inhales four cups (one liter) of other people's gases every day.

Speaking of

... you're full of it. After you eat and drink, your body **extracts** the nutrients from your feast.

The rest is turned into poop. Human **intestines** are about the length of a garden hose. How much poop can fit in a garden hose? A lot.

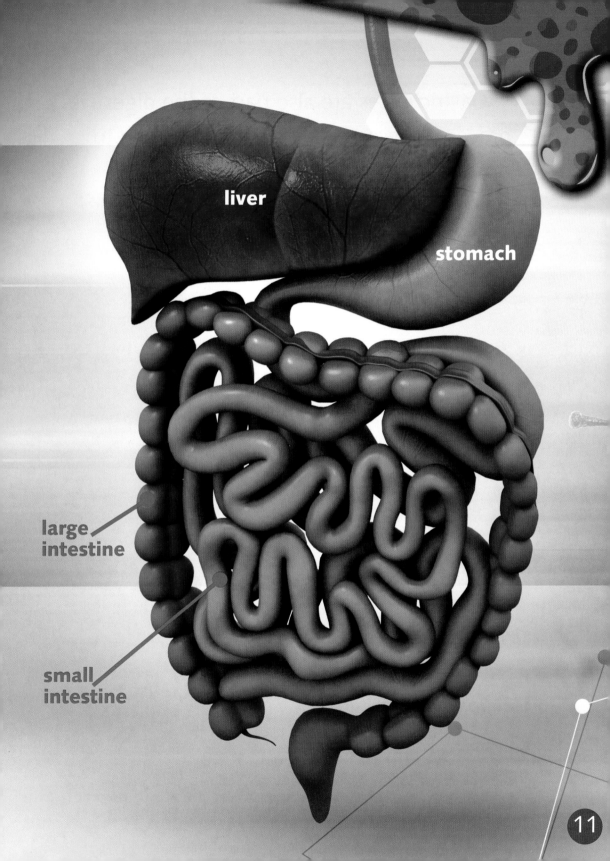

liver

stomach

large intestine

small intestine

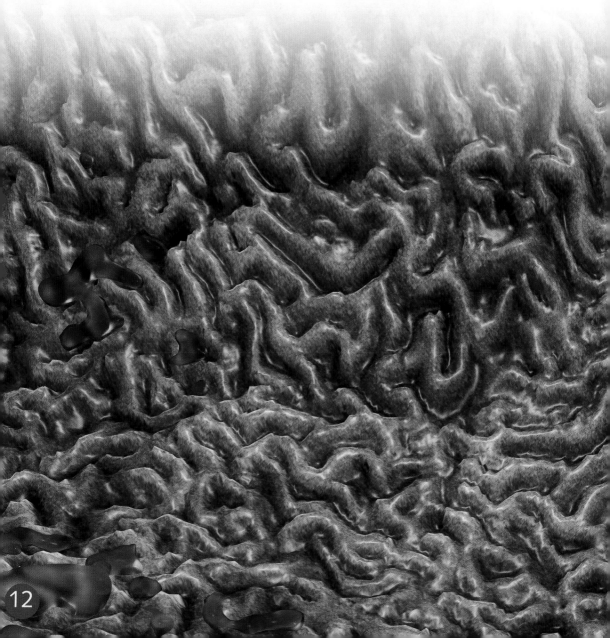

Gastric juices are also part of the digestive process. These acids are strong enough to dissolve razor blades. They are gross and powerful!

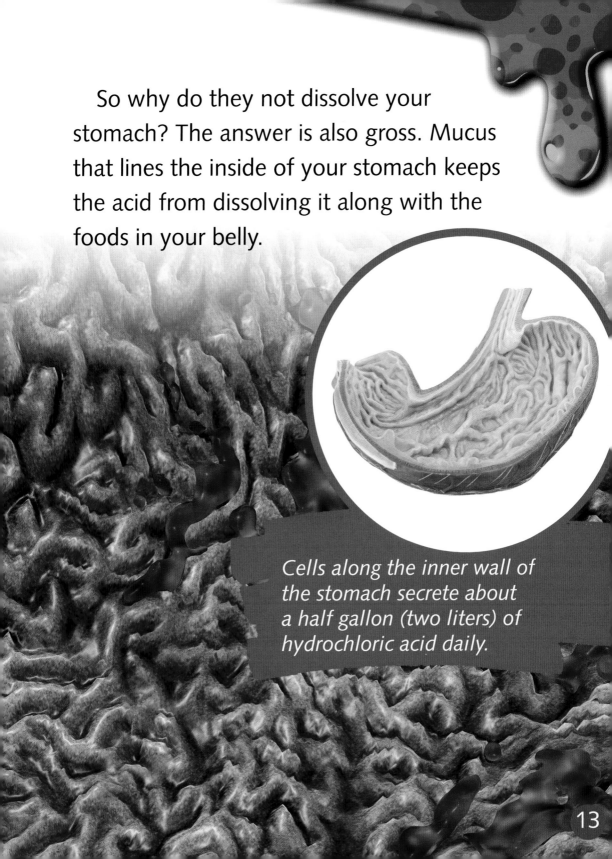

So why do they not dissolve your stomach? The answer is also gross. Mucus that lines the inside of your stomach keeps the acid from dissolving it along with the foods in your belly.

Cells along the inner wall of the stomach secrete about a half gallon (two liters) of hydrochloric acid daily.

GOOD AND GOOEY

Mucus is everywhere in your body, actually. This slimy substance coats the inside of your mouth, nose, sinuses, throat, lungs, and **gastrointestinal** tract. It keeps your body tissues from drying out.

This sticky goo also traps bacteria, dirt, pollen, and other **airborne** gunk. Your snot and boogers are like tiny trash bags, full of debris your body doesn't want.

Tiny hair-like muscles, called cilia, line your nasal passage and airway. The cilia team up with the mucus to trap and move airborne gunk toward your stomach, where the acid destroys it.

15

Your eyes have their own goo, too. You know that crud in the corners of your eyes when you first wake up? It's a type of rheum called gound. When you're awake, you blink away the gound. It builds up while you're sleeping because you're not blinking.

Bacterial infections can make your eye goo even gooier. It gets thicker and yellow. This means it's time to see a doctor!

Rheum is a thin mucus secretion that comes from our eyes, noses and mouths. It is made up of mucus, skin cells, oils, and dust. Gound may be wet and sticky or dry and crusty.

A runny nose can be caused by anything that irritates nasal tissues. Pet dander, pollen, smoke, and bacterial infections can turn your nose into a snot faucet!

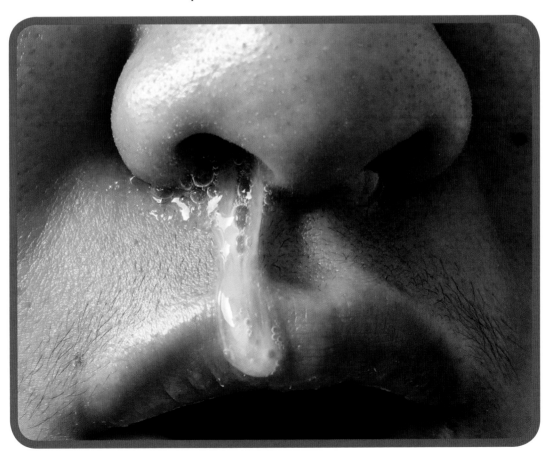

If mucus keeps stuff out of your nose, mouth, and eyes, what's protecting your ears? Cerumen, also known as earwax. These secretions protect your ear canals from invaders, like snot does in your nose.

There are two kinds of earwax. One is brown, sticky, and wet. The other is gray, dry, and flaky. Wet earwax is more common in people of European and African descent. Dry earwax is more common in people of Asian and Native American descent.

wet earwax

FARTS, BURPS, AND PUKE

Earwax may be different, depending on your ancestry, but when it comes to burping and farting, we are all the same. We are passing this gas from our mouths and rears at least 14 times a day. That adds up to between three and six cups (237 to 710 milliliters) daily.

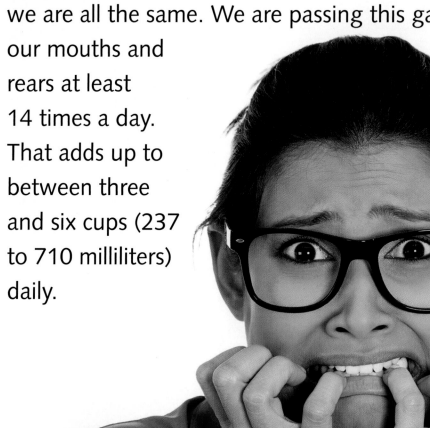

Most of your farts come from swallowing air while you eat and drink. Gas is also produced by your body as it digests food.

Much of the gas you pass from swallowed air is made up of nitrogen and carbon dioxide.

Some foods cause more gas than others. Beans, eggs, and other foods have sugars in them that the human body does not digest well. When they get to your intestines undigested, bacteria attacks.

Gut bacteria gobble up unused foods, then churn out gas. Some say being gassy is a sign of good health. Toot toot!

These bacteria are what gives your farts their stink. Bacteria farts contain **methane** and **hydrogen**. This makes them flammable!

So you've just finished a huge meal. You burp, you fart, and you still feel too full to move. And maybe a little queasy.

A human stomach can hold about three quarters of a gallon (three liters) of food and liquids. But what happens if your stomach and intestines can't handle what you've sent their way?

3/4 Gallon = 6 pints

It's coming back up. Vomiting happens when food can't be digested properly. The muscles in your stomach and intestines push the food up instead of down and carry it back where it started.

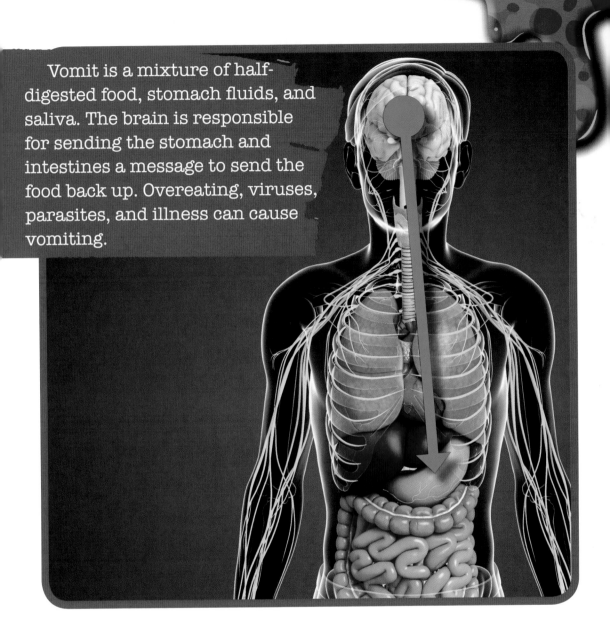

Vomit is a mixture of half-digested food, stomach fluids, and saliva. The brain is responsible for sending the stomach and intestines a message to send the food back up. Overeating, viruses, parasites, and illness can cause vomiting.

No matter how clean and polite we try to be, our bodies are always doing some pretty gross stuff.

Sometimes we don't notice. Other times, the proof is in your nostrils!

GROSS, BUT TRUE

Human mouths contain between 500 and 1,000 types of bacteria.

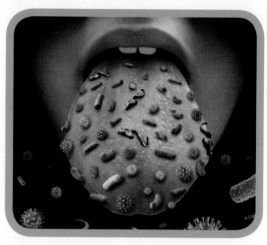

Our sinuses make about 34 ounces (one liter) of mucus every day.

The human body produces two to four pints (.95 to 1.9 liters) of saliva per day. That's enough to fill two swimming pools in an average lifetime.

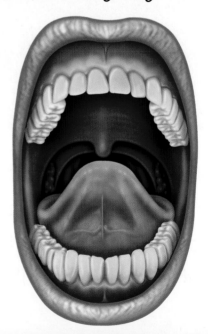

Each of your feet has more than 250,000 sweat glands and can produce more than a pint (.5 liters) of sweat per day.

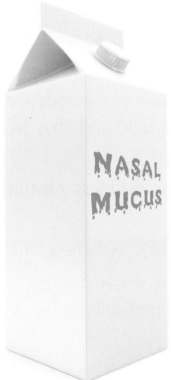

NASAL MUCUS

Humans swallow about a quart (.95 liters) of nasal mucus, or snot, every day.

Your urine is sterile and cleaner than your saliva. It's even cleaner than tap water! But only until it leaves your body and comes in contact with bacteria.

GLOSSARY

airborne (air-born): transported by air

extracts (EK-STRACKTS): removing or pulling something out

gastrointestinal (gas-TROH-in-test-in-uhl): relating to the stomach and the intestines

hydrogen (HYE-druh-juhn): a gas with no smell or color that is lighter than air and catches fire easily

intestines (in-TES-tins): a long tube in the body extending below the stomach that digests food and absorbs liquids and salts

methane (METH-ane): a colorless, odorless gas that burns easily and is used for fuel

microscopic (mye-kruh-SKAH-pik): extremely small

molecules (MAH-luh-kyools): the smallest unit a chemical compound can be divided into that still displays all of its chemical properties

INDEX

SHOW WHAT YOU KNOW

1. How do bacteria help keep people healthy?
2. What is the purpose of snot?
3. What must happen for you to be able to smell something?
4. How much gas does the average person pass every day?
5. What makes gas flammable?

WEBSITES TO VISIT

www.ngkids.co.uk/science-and-nature/15-facts-about-the-human-body

http://kidshealth.org/kid/talk/yucky/puke.html

http://easyscienceforkids.com/bacteria-good-guy-or-bad-guy/

About the Author

Darla Duhaime is a writer and purveyor of strange—and gross—facts from Sheffield, Vermont. When she's not writing, she enjoys picking wild berries, daydreaming, and cloud-watching. She likes to stay active and is known for keeping things interesting at family gatherings.

Meet The Author!
www.meetREMauthors.com

www.rourkeeducationalmedia.com

PHOTO CREDITS: Cover: demodex mite © Kalcutta, boy © rmnoa357, intestines © Christos Georghiou, background © Ihnatovich Maryia; page 4: Gross Me Out Letters © Cory Thoman; page 4 boy © saisnaps, page 5 © Kalcutta; page 6 bacteria © Doc. RNDr. Josef Reischig, CSc., yoghurt © Olga Popova, page 7 intestines © Christos Georghiou; page 8 poop icon © Sudowoodo, page 9 smell vapors © corbac40, boy © Asier Romero; page 10 word poop © Tony Oshlick, hose © IhorZigor, page 11 © Horoscope; page 12-13 © UGREEN 3S, page 13 inset © Ben Schonewille; page 15 © sumroeng chinnapan; page 16 © charnsitr, page 17 © Bill paptawan; page 18-19 © NorGal, page 18 inset © kzww; page 20 © PathDoc, page 21 top © alexeyulanov, cartoon © chompoo; page 22 © darqdesign, page 23 © Designua, girl © PathDoc; page 24-25 © Carlos Caetano, page 25 milk cartons © cigdem; page 26 © blambca, page 27© S K Chavan; page 28 top and middle © Lightspring, bottom © Alexilusmedical; page 29 top © corbac40, middle © Rashevskyi Viacheslav, bottom © Tom Schoumakers All images from Shutterstock.com except bacteria page 6

Edited by: Keli Sipperley

Cover and Interior design by: Nicola Stratford   www.nicolastratford.com

Library of Congress PCN Data

Gross Body Stuff / Darla Duhaime
(Gross Me Out!)
 ISBN 978-1-68191-767-2 (hard cover)
 ISBN 978-1-68191-868-6 (soft cover)
 ISBN 978-1-68191-956-0 (e-Book)
Library of Congress Control Number: 2016932727

Rourke Educational Media
Printed in the United States of America, North Mankato, Minnesota

Also Available as:
ROURKE'S
e-Books

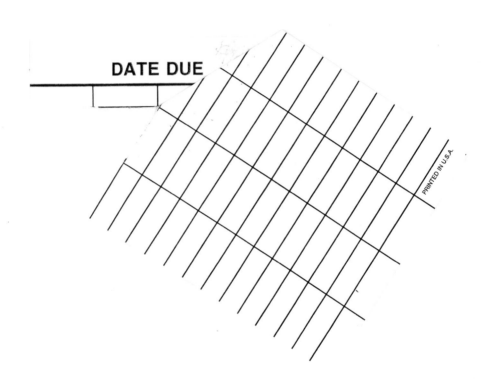

DATE DUE